Travel Journal

Thailand

VPJournals

Contact Details

Name: _____

Email address: _____

Tel: _____

Address: _____

_____

_____

Important Medical Information

Blood type: _____

Medication: _____

CONTENTS

Hi, I hope you enjoy this journal. It is packed with cool stuff and recommendations for you trip to Thailand, and has plenty of space to record details of your trip.

Have fun in Thailand

Great Places to visit in Thailand

The Grand Palace	✓
Wat Phra Kaew	
Nong Nooch Tropical Botanical Garden	
Freedom Beach	
Phranang Full Moon Kayaking	
Banyan Golf Club	
Phanom Rung	
Railay	
Khao Sok National Park	
Ayuthaya	
Kanchanaburi	

Amphawa Floating Market	
The Ancient City	
Erawan Museum	
Madame Tussauds Wax Museum	
Royal Barges Museum	
Siam Ocean World Bangkok	
Wat Arun	
Wat Pho in Bangkok	
Vimanmek Mansion	
Taling Chan Floating Market	
Bangkok National Museum	
Siam Park City	
Flower Market (Pak Klong Talad)	

Cool Places to visit in Thailand with Kids

Safari World	✓
Kidzania Bangkok	
Siam Park City	
Fantasia Lagoon	
Siam Ocean World	
Dream World	
Madame Tussauds Wax Museum	
Flow Rider	
Funarium Indoor Playground	
Kidzooonia at Gateway Mall	
Art in Paradise	
Snake Farm	

Dusit Zoo	
Leoland Water Park	
Butterfly Garden & Insectarium	
Lumpini Park	
Bangkok National Museum	
Erawan Museum	
Flight Experience Bangkok	
Flower Market (Pak Klong Talad)	
The Grand Palace	
Amphawa Floating Market	
The Ancient City	
Freedom Beach	

Good Places to Eat in **Thailand**

Lenzi Tuscan Kitchen	✔
Nang Gin Kui - Bangkok Private Dining	
Rock Restaurant and Bar	
Le Normandie Restaurant at Mandarin Oriental, Bangkok	
Tealicious Bangkok	
G's Bangkok	
The Living Room	
Brio	
L'Appart Sofitel Bangkok Sukhumvit	
Old Town Cafe Bangkok	

JP French Restaurant	
Seven Spoons Bar and Restaurant	
Teuscher Chocolates of Switzerland & Cocoa Lounge - Thailand	
Scalini	
Issaya Siamese Club	
Le Du Restaurant	
Le Beaulieu at Plaza Athenee	
Bo Lan	
Nahm	
Elements At Okura Prestige Hotel	
Maverick Restaurant & Bar	

Best Websites to Research Further

Do some more research on the internet to plan your trip:

www.thailander.com
www.tourismthailand.org
www.lonelyplanet.com/Thailand
www.nationsonline.org/oneworld/thailand.htm
www.guidetothailand.com
www.bangkok.com
www.thaizer.com
www.wikipedia.org/wiki/Thailand
www.nomadicmatt.com/travel-guides/Thailand-travel-tips/

More places I want to visit on our trip

1. _____
2. _____
3. _____
4. _____
5. _____
6. _____
7. _____
8. _____
9. _____
10. _____
11. _____
12. _____
13. _____
14. _____
15. _____

Postcard List

Name:
Address:

Name:
Address:

Name:
Address:

Name:

Address:

Name:

Address:

Name:

Address:

Name:

Address:

Name:

Address:

Name:

Address:

Name:

Address:

Name:

Address:

Name:

Address:

Name:

Address:

Name:

Address:

MAIL

Packing List

✓	This Journal
	Tickets
	Passport
	Money
	Chargers
	Batteries
	Book to read
	Camera
	Tablet
	Sun glasses
	Sun cream

	Toiletries
	Water
	Watch
	Snacks
	Umbrella
	Towel
	Guide book
	Kindle
	Jacket
	Medication
	Add more below

Thailand Facts

- The official name of Thailand is the Kingdom of Thailand, it was formerly known as Siam until 1939 (and again from 1945 to 1949)

- Thailand has a land border with four countries including Myanmar (formerly Burma), Laos, Cambodia and Malaysia. It's coastline is 3,219 km long

- Thailand has a population of 67 million people. Bangkok is the largest city and the capital of Thailand

- Thailand has over 1,430 islands

- Buddhism is the primary religion in Thailand; it is practiced by about 95% of the population. Throughout Thailand are many Buddhist temples and grand golden Buddhist statues

- Siamese cats originated in Thailand where they are called Wichian Mat

- Thailand's national symbol is the elephant. A century ago there were 100,000 elephants in the country, now there are only an estimated 2,000 left in the wild

- Muay Thai (Thai boxing) is a form of kickboxing and is Thailand's national sport, it is known as "the art of the eight limbs".

- Thailand is often called the "Golf Capital of Asia", with beautifully kept courses at a reasonable price the country attracts a larger number of golfers from around the world

- Kitti's hog-nosed bat, thought to be the world's smallest mammal, is found in Thailand. It weights just two grams

- It is against the law to criticise the monarchy in Thailand

- Thailand's highest point is Doi Inthanon in the Thanon Thong Chai mountain range

- In Thailand, it is illegal to leave your house without underwear on

- Bangkok once had dozens of canals and it's buildings stood on stilts. Most of these canals have now been filled

Clothes & Shoe Sizes

Children's Shoe Sizes

UK	EUROPE	US	Japan
4	20	4½ or 5	12 ½
4 ½	21	5 or 5½	13
5	21 or 22	5½ or 6	13 ½
5 ½	22	6	13½ or 14
6	23	6½ or 7	14 or 14½
6 ½	23 or 24	7 ½	14½ or 15
7	24	7½ or 8	15
7 ½	25	8 or 9	15 ½
8	25 or 26	8½ or 9	16
8 ½	26	9½	16 ½
9	27	9½ or 10	16 ½ or 17
10	28	10½ or 11	17 ½
10½ or 11	29	11½ or 12	18
11 ½	30	12½	18 or 18 ½
12	31	13	19 or 19 ½
12 ½	31	13 or 13½	19 ½ or 20
13	32	1	20
13 ½	32 ½	1 ½	20 ½
1	33	1½ or 2	21
2	34	2½ or 3	22

Children's Clothing Sizes

UK	EUROPE	US	Australia
12m	80cm	12-18m	12m
18m	80-86cm	18-24m	18m
24m	86-92cm	23-24m	2
2-3	92-98cm	2T	3
3-4	98-104cm	4T	4
3-5	104-110cm	5	5
5-6	110-116cm	6	6
6-7	116-122cm	6X-7	7
7-8	122-128cm	7 to 8	8
8-9	128-134cm	9 to 10	9
9-10	134-140cm	10	10
10-11	140-146cm	11	11
11-12	146-152cm	14	12

Women's Shoe Sizes

UK	EUROPE	US	Japan
3	35 ½	5	22 ½
3 ½	36	5 ½	23
4	37	6	23
4 ½	37 ½	6 ½	23 ½
5	38	7	24
5 ½	39	7 ½	24
6	39 ½	8	24 ½
6 ½	40	8 ½	25
7	41	9 ½	25 ½
7 ½	41 ½	10	26
8	42	10 ½	26 ½

Women's Clothes Sizes

UK	US	Japan	France / Spain	Germany	Thailand	Australia
6/8	6	7-9	36	34	40	8
10	8	9-11	38	36	42	10
12	10	11-13	40	38	44	12
14	12	13-15	42	39	46	14
16	14	15-17	44	40	48	16
18	16	17-19	46	42	50	18
20	18	19-21	48	44	52	20

Men's Shoe Sizes

UK	EUROPE	US	Japan
6	38 ½	6 ½	24 ½
6 ½	39	7	25
7	40	7 ½	25 ½
7 ½	41	8	26
8	42	8 ½	27 ½
8 ½	43	9	27 ½
9	43 ½	9 ½	28
9 ½	44	10	28 ½
10	44	10 ½	28 ½
10 ½	44 ½	11	29
11	45	12	29 ½

Men's Suit / Coat / Sweater Sizes

UK / US / Aus	EU / Japan	General
32	42	Small
34	44	Small
36	46	Small
38	48	Medium
40	50	Large
42	52	Large
44	54	Extra Large
46	56	Extra Large

Men's Pants / Trouser Sizes (Waist)

UK / US	Europe
32	81 cm
34	86 cm
36	91 cm
38	97 cm
40	102 cm
42	107 cm

We have included another copy of this at the back of the book, so you can find it quickly again when you are in Thailand

Thailand Trip Diary

Write a daily diary during your trip

Day 1

Date: _____ **Weather:** _____

Day 2

Date: _____   **Weather:** _____

Day 3

Date: _____   **Weather:** _____

_____

_____

_____

_____

_____

_____

_____

_____

_____

_____

_____

_____

_____

_____

Day 4

Date: _____   **Weather:** _____

_____

_____

_____

_____

_____

_____

_____

_____

_____

_____

_____

_____

_____

_____

Day 5

Date: _____   **Weather:** _____

_____

_____

_____

_____

_____

_____

_____

_____

_____

_____

_____

_____

_____

_____

Day 6

Date: _____   **Weather:** _____

_____

_____

_____

_____

_____

_____

_____

_____

_____

_____

_____

_____

_____

Day 7

Date: _____   **Weather:** _____

_____

_____

_____

_____

_____

_____

_____

_____

_____

_____

_____

_____

_____

_____

Day 8

Date: _____   **Weather:** _____

_____

_____

_____

_____

_____

_____

_____

_____

_____

_____

_____

_____

_____

_____

_____

_____

_____

_____

Day 9

Date: _____   **Weather:** _____

_____

_____

_____

_____

_____

_____

_____

_____

_____

_____

_____

_____

_____

_____

_____

Day 10

Date: _____   **Weather:** _____

_____

_____

_____

_____

_____

_____

_____

_____

_____

_____

_____

_____

_____

_____

_____

_____

Day 11

Date: _____　　　**Weather:** _____

Day 12

Date: _____   **Weather:** _____

_____

_____

_____

_____

_____

_____

_____

_____

_____

_____

_____

_____

_____

_____

_____

_____

Day 13

Date: _____   **Weather:** _____

_____

_____

_____

_____

_____

_____

_____

_____

_____

_____

_____

_____

_____

_____

_____

Day 14

Date: _____   **Weather:** _____

Day 15

Date: _____   **Weather:** _____

Day 16

Date: _____ **Weather:** _____

_____

_____

_____

_____

_____

_____

_____

_____

_____

_____

_____

_____

_____

Day 17

Date: _____   **Weather:** _____

Day 18

Date: _____ **Weather:** _____

_____

_____

_____

_____

_____

_____

_____

_____

_____

_____

_____

_____

_____

Day 19

Date: _____   **Weather:** _____

_____

_____

_____

_____

_____

_____

_____

_____

_____

_____

_____

_____

_____

Day 20

Date: _____   **Weather:** _____

_____

_____

_____

_____

_____

_____

_____

_____

_____

_____

_____

_____

_____

_____

_____

_____

Day 21

Date: _____   **Weather:** _____

_____

_____

_____

_____

_____

_____

_____

_____

_____

_____

_____

_____

_____

_____

_____

Memories of your Trip

Things I will remember from the trip

Favorite Places visited on the Trip

People I Met

Name:	
Address:	
Tel:	
email:	

Name:	
Address:	
Tel:	
email:	

Name:	
Address:	
Tel:	
email:	

Name:
Address:
Tel:
email:

Name:
Address:
Tel:
email:

Name:
Address:
Tel:
email:

Name:
Address:
Tel:
email:

Name:
Address:
Tel:
email:

Name:
Address:
Tel:
email:

Name:
Address:
Tel:
email:

Name:
Address:
Tel:
email:

We hope you enjoyed your trip to Thailand

Please leave us a review if you found this Journal useful

Check out our useful resources on the next few pages

Clothes & Shoe Sizes

Children's Shoe Sizes

UK	EUROPE	US	Japan
4	20	4½ or 5	12 ½
4 ½	21	5 or 5½	13
5	21 or 22	5½ or 6	13 ½
5 ½	22	6	13½ or 14
6	23	6½ or 7	14 or 14½
6 ½	23 or 24	7 ½	14½ or 15
7	24	7½ or 8	15
7 ½	25	8 or 9	15 ½
8	25 or 26	8½ or 9	16
8 ½	26	9½	16 ½
9	27	9½ or 10	16 ½ or 17
10	28	10½ or 11	17 ½
10½ or 11	29	11½ or 12	18
11 ½	30	12½	18 or 18 ½
12	31	13	19 or 19 ½
12 ½	31	13 or 13½	19 ½ or 20
13	32	1	20
13 ½	32 ½	1 ½	20 ½
1	33	1½ or 2	21
2	34	2½ or 3	22

Children's Clothing Sizes

UK	EUROPE	US	Australia
12m	80cm	12-18m	12m
18m	80-86cm	18-24m	18m
24m	86-92cm	23-24m	2
2-3	92-98cm	2T	3
3-4	98-104cm	4T	4
3-5	104-110cm	5	5
5-6	110-116cm	6	6
6-7	116-122cm	6X-7	7
7-8	122-128cm	7 to 8	8
8-9	128-134cm	9 to 10	9
9-10	134-140cm	10	10
10-11	140-146cm	11	11
11-12	146-152cm	14	12

Women's Shoe Sizes

UK	EUROPE	US	Japan
3	35 ½	5	22 ½
3 ½	36	5 ½	23
4	37	6	23
4 ½	37 ½	6 ½	23 ½
5	38	7	24
5 ½	39	7 ½	24
6	39 ½	8	24 ½
6 ½	40	8 ½	25
7	41	9 ½	25 ½
7 ½	41 ½	10	26
8	42	10 ½	26 ½

Women's Clothes Sizes

UK	US	Japan	France / Spain	Germany	Thailand	Australia
6/8	6	7-9	36	34	40	8
10	8	9-11	38	36	42	10
12	10	11-13	40	38	44	12
14	12	13-15	42	39	46	14
16	14	15-17	44	40	48	16
18	16	17-19	46	42	50	18
20	18	19-21	48	44	52	20

Men's Shoe Sizes

UK	EUROPE	US	Japan
6	38 ½	6 ½	24 ½
6 ½	39	7	25
7	40	7 ½	25 ½
7 ½	41	8	26
8	42	8 ½	27 ½
8 ½	43	9	27 ½
9	43 ½	9 ½	28
9 ½	44	10	28 ½
10	44	10 ½	28 ½
10 ½	44 ½	11	29
11	45	12	29 ½

Men's Suit / Coat / Sweater Sizes

UK / US / Aus	EU / Japan	General
32	42	Small
34	44	Small
36	46	Small
38	48	Medium
40	50	Large
42	52	Large
44	54	Extra Large
46	56	Extra Large

Men's Pants / Trouser Sizes (Waist)

UK / US	Europe
32	81 cm
34	86 cm
36	91 cm
38	97 cm
40	102 cm
42	107 cm

Common Translations

English	French	Spanish	Italian
Hello	Bonjour	Hola	Ciao
Goodbye	Au revoir	Adiós	Arrivederci
Yes	Oui	Sí	Si
No	Non	No	No
Please	S'il-vous-plaît	Por favor	Per favore
Thank you	Merci	Gracias	Grazie
Excuse me	Excusez-moi	Perdón	Mi scusi
How much	Combien	Cuánto	Quanto
My name is	Mon nom est	Mi nombre es	Io mi chiamo
Where is	Où est	Dónde está	Dov'è
The bank	La banque	El banco	La banca
The toilet	Les toilettes	El baño	Il bagno

German	Japanese	Mandarin	Hindi
Hallo	Kon'nichiwa	Ni hao	Namaste
Auf Wiedersehen	Sayonara	Zaijian	Alavida
Ja	Hai	Shi de	Ham
Nein	Ie	Meiyou	Nahim
Bitte	Onegaishimasu	Qing	Krpaya
Vielen Dank	Arigato	Xiexie	Dhan'yavada
Entschuldigung	Sumimasen	Duoshao	Mujhe mapha karem
Wie viel	Ikura	Wo de mingzi shi	Kitana
Mein Name ist	Watashinonamaeha	Nali	Mera nama hai
Wo ist	Doko ni aru	Yinhang	Kaham hai
Die Bank	Ginko	Yinhang	Bainka
Die Toilette	Toire	Cesuo	Saucalaya

Notes:

Made in the USA
San Bernardino, CA
11 December 2016